I0087835

BEHΩLD
poems

Michael McCarthy

With artist Kimberly Callas

RESOURCE *Publications* · Eugene, Oregon

BEHOLD
Poems

Copyright © 2024 Michael McCarthy. All rights reserved. Except for brief quotations in critical publications or reviews, no part of this book may be reproduced in any manner without prior written permission from the publisher. Write: Permissions, Wipf and Stock Publishers, 199 W. 8th Ave., Suite 3, Eugene, OR 97401.

Resource Publications
An Imprint of Wipf and Stock Publishers
199 W. 8th Ave., Suite 3
Eugene, OR 97401

www.wipfandstock.com

PAPERBACK ISBN: 979-8-3852-3939-9
HARDCOVER ISBN: 979-8-3852-3940-5
EBOOK ISBN: 979-8-3852-3941-2

Tell them, I am love

I gratefully acknowledge the editors of two wonderful literary journals, in which some of these poems first appeared, sometimes in slightly different form: *Southern Review*: "Beneath," "Kepler's Song," and "Grace and Gravity" (as "Autumnal"); and *Poetry East*: "Spiral Staircase," "On My Birth Certificate," and "Etch a Sketch."

*The greatest of joy
is to behold God
in all things.*

Julian of Norwich

Table of Contents

Introduction: The Heavens Declare 1

Parabola 7

Arch 8

Life Span 10

Archetype 12

Saint Louis Arch 15

Space in Man 24

Whispering Arch 25

Priory Church 26

Water Music 28

Brushstroke 32

Hyperbola 33

One Giant Leap 35

My Guitar 36

Foot Notes 37

Lamplight 39

Spiral Staircase 40

Beneath 41

On My Birth Certificate 43

Spirit of St. Louis 44

little redhead 46

Ellipse 49

Ode to Joy 51

Kepler's Song 52

Dust 53

Mark Twain 54

Etch a Sketch 56

The Discovery of Neptune 57

Heavengravel 58

Spirals 66

Seeds 68

Cone 69

Teepee 71
Turning Triangle 73
Findspot 74
Oracles 76
Let Us Make 78
Sittings..79
Over and Over..81
Grace and Gravity 83
be hold 84

Notes..86

Introduction: The Heavens Declare

How being bends. Into celestial bodies. Into our bodies.

Space and humanity are blood relatives, sharing a common ancestry in a family of primal curves. These simple, familiar curves shape the narrative arc of our origin story, from the beginning of our world to the evolution and form of human beings and language.

Surprisingly, the cosmos and people so share the same blueprint that we may need a new word to describe this harmony. Maybe *cosmortal*. With energy and spirit, geometry courses within us and without us. It flows in circles, ellipses, parabolas and hyperbolas. Through elliptical orbits, trillions of dust particles converged around our Sun into larger clumps, then into boulders, and eventually into planets. Over four billion years ago, the ellipse put the Earth on the path to life.

On that whirling globe, a remarkable new creature curled forth. Over three million years ago, an anatomical novelty arose in the feet of our ancestors. Hyperbolas of ligament and bone allowed them to stand upright and walk around habitually, decisively transforming hominids into modern people. Into us.

Into us even further, as we broke from the past with the sculpting of the modern, compact chin. With the elegant parabolas of our teeth and jaws, speech became possible, and language flowered forth. We could not possibly have become the human beings we are, a growing body of evidence shows, without the parabola and hyperbola first shaping our anatomy.

The traits of walking and talking distinguish us, anthropologists say, from every other animal in the kingdom. And, then it suddenly struck me—comets and asteroids journey in the exact same arches that define our mouths and feet. Imagine, smiles and footprints in the sky. Our passing bones are tuned to heavenly bodies that keep time in eons.

An inborn recognition stirs, it seems, when you see tree branches bent in an arc, or waves roll on the ocean, an intimacy like the twists of your signature, or the timbre of your mother's voice. Feel the contours of your teeth now, the soles of your feet. We are arches incarnate.

I grew up in the heartland city of St. Louis in the 1960s, when these beautiful curves emerged in science and art. It was a Space Age capital, where scientists including my father turned trajectories into moonshots. At the same time, a glory of arches arose from the flatland. The shiny skyscraper of the St. Louis Arch, notably, and the round cake of parabolas that composed my Priory School church. The silence within.

So began the call. My poetic response of the past dozen years took me from anthropology to astrophysics, and across the globe. To Rome, the empire built on arches. To Utah, where nature is sculpted in Arches National Park. To Sámos, the Greek isle of Pythagoras, who opened doors with triangles. This journey helped me to speak a language I had not known before.

The sky has enlightened earlier explorers of curvature. In the 17th century, the German astronomer Kepler discovered that planets orbit in ellipses. His Italian contemporary, Galileo, found that every object lobbed travels in a parabola, from an arrow flying to a dolphin leaping. Over two millennia ago, mathematical mystics edged toward the numinous when they discovered that these curves could all be produced from a single source, one object. A cone.

A cone? Think of a teepee, a funnel, a volcano. Slice it one way, a parabola forms in the cross section; another, an ellipse. And so on. Ellipse, parabola, hyperbola. The conic sections. Every single object in the heavens orbits in one of these shapes—and only in these shapes. No other.

Why was the cone so motherly, I wondered, such a wellspring of curves shaping matter into planets and people? For years, I searched. At last, I turned to Euclid, the Greek geometer. The cone is defined, he wrote, by taking a triangle and rotating it around. Spin a musical triangle on its string, it forms a cone. So the triangle, the generator of the cone, is a root of material being. The triangle, our family of origin.

Trigonometry, the study of triangles, has long illuminated realities from sound waves to light and electricity. And the offspring of the triangle, the precise and symmetric oval and arch sections of the cone, are the defining geometry not just of outer space, but of humanity as well. The faraway is actually deep within. Slices of the same whole. Along with the heavens and the earth, we are, every one of the eight billion souls here, one race, one blood. Put another way, there is no *them*, there is only us.

For the next connection, I credit grace. In Christian theology, the essence of God is revealed as threefold, a Father, a Son and a Holy Spirit. That sacred Trinity has been portrayed throughout history as a triangle.

People have long spotted patterns, repetition and elegant shapes throughout nature, in the sky, in the sea, throughout the land. They have intuited some design of God, a Sacred Geometry. With his famous, limb-spread Vitruvian Man, Leonardo da Vinci sketched beautiful ratios of human anatomy within a square and circle.

We've struck upon a previously untold origin story here, though. The Arch Mortal. Through the curves of the divinely stirring cone, all human beings came to be. And without them, not a single one has come to be. The cone, in turn, links us to the heavens.

Not as a trained scientist do I see space and humanity as blood relatives, but as a stargazer and a poet, hoping to trace a chain of truth. It could be an intentional harmony of design and beauty between us and the cosmos, this loom of origins. Or it could merely be incredible coincidence amid chaos. I approach with a child's wonder. Flowers for eyes. We seem to share a striking family resemblance with God.

The grand book, the universe ... is written in the language of mathematics, and its characters are triangles, circles, and other geometric figures, without which it is humanly impossible to understand a single word of it...

Galileo

Parabola

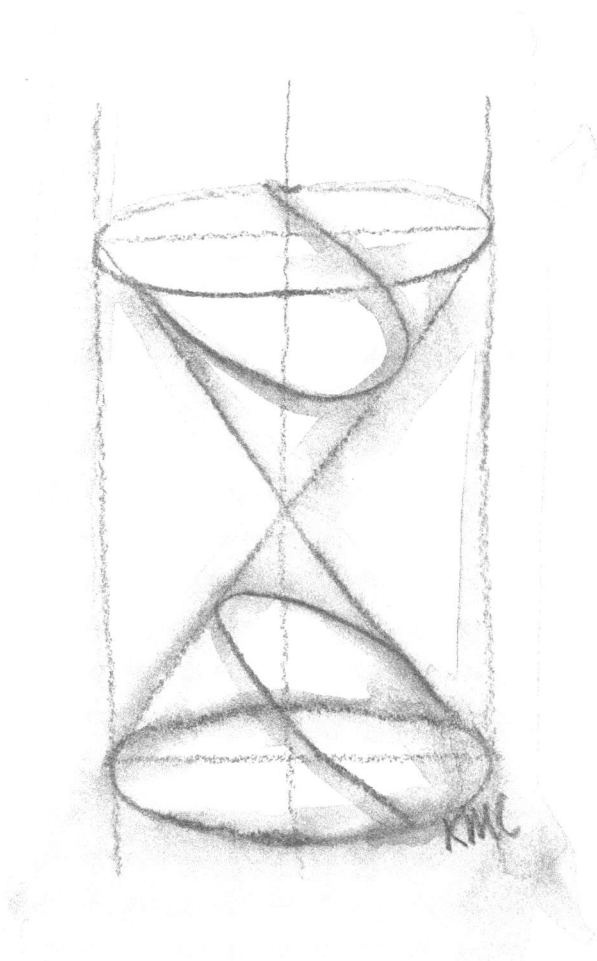

Arch

A graceful curve
incarnate in cheeks,
an array of stones,
not bones, stronger;
stronger than gold
or iron, teeth so hard
they persist a million
years and more in the
fossil record, a sculpted
rock garden, incarnate
in a sweeping arc
echoing the great
orbits of the planets,
a harmony of design
so unmistakable,
an arcade of teeth,
older than Stonehenge,
formed eon upon eon,

eons upon eons
little stone arches
bridging perhaps right
and left hemispheres
of the brain, a trace of
infinity in every mouth,
the vital doorway through
which every word ever
spoken in every language
ever spoken could finally
form and pass, a resonating
chamber so unique to people,
to humankind, that it defines
us as us, and allows me
to speak to you, even now,
of a bigger story, hidden
right there all this time
right under your nose.

Life Span

Delicate Arch rises
above the deserts
of North America
a bow in the clouds.

Bending likeness
toward essence
this stone arc stands
for all of humanity.

The only true voyage
of discovery, it was once
said, is not in seeking new
lands but in having new eyes.

Bony arches elevated
the human species,
undergirding miracles
called walking, talking

and this stone span
unites the arches of
jaws and feet to render
a mouth standing.

Rainbow of rock
hewn open by gravity
and water, absence
creating presence.

The more the marble
wastes, Michelangelo
taught us, *the more*
the statue grows.

To see any upright arch
is to see every person
ever born, to see
a temple of template

both rising and falling
in a covenant of peace
built at bedrock
to open and connect.

The Arch in Australia
Moon Hill in Asia
Pon d'Arc in Europe
Aloba Arch in Africa

how naturally they all
resemble the Omega
Ω the Greek for finale,
or the end of a series,

as if humanity were
the promised land
of a grandeur built on
an invisible speck called

hydrogen, which created
stars, then elements, then
planets, then flowers, and,
given enough time, people.

Ω

Archetype

Stacked in stone
ancient arches
evoke order
the world is too
much with us
to see.

So we long

for their
symmetry
fluid ecstasy
unity in variety
sunrise and sunfall
loop of life
rising from soil
returning to it,
above all
silent shapes
from beyond,
parables that
someone else
is always leaning
in alongside us.

With eyes drawn
skyward from
the blinking bedlam in our hands,
people carried away, twisting
in fictions, wary of other,
hope curls forth
in sky scrapers of old
lessons beyond
wrinkles. As arches
arches never rest.

Rome planted arches
all over the empire,
and one from antiquity
stands nearly intact
while the Colosseum's
arena of games nearby
is two-thirds gone
and less still survives
from the old court
of Rome, the Forum.

An indelicate arch on the surface
this remaining relic is a tower
of triumph for a given emperor
but the feet
it stands on
were shaped by
unseen forces of
nature, assembled
not in defiance
of gravity, but in
an arc of covenant
between rise and fall.

Its graceful form
persists while time
corrodes its crosswise carvings
of conquest, of force, of spoils,
of people carried away,
leaving an accidental elegy,
a tombstone to self,
and a lasting
testament to
larger life spans.

A continent away
a memorial to waves,
a sea of stone arches,
arises in St. Louis
crafted by a sculptor
with limestone formed
when the whole of
Midwest America
was undersea, two dozen
quarried arches dance
in waves evoking wind
over water, in a primal
rise and fall and reach
for the sky. Arches, like
souls, never rest.

St. Louis Arch

cloud

                sun
   flash

   sky tower curl

wave   wave   wave

mud rock rock rock road

trickle   ripples   trickle

Today was our
field trip,
all the
second graders.
My eyes watered
looking up.
The arch is up
in the clouds.
Our teacher told us
it is very new.
I said I thought it
was always there.
She laughed
and laughed,
and then told
the other teacher,
Now I feel old,
really old.

I reach out to the silver leg. It is cold.
It feels like one of Mom's pots.

I smell licorice. Dad loves licorice.
A candy factory is on the river.

We learned to spell the river
in school singing, *M i SS i SS i PP i*

I hear the water splash on the cobblestones.
They are hard to run on fast.

I licked the arch when I was little, my Dad
says, saying it tasted like Mom's cake beaters.

My Dad takes a photo of us. I am looking
away from him, looking at the arch.

My little sister holds my big sister's hand.
One is in first grade, the other eighth.

The arch looks like a rainbow. Or a wishbone
my sisters and I pull apart. Both are for luck.

The arch seems like it has always been.

Thirty now, on a trip
with my son and daughter.
Eleven hours by car,

we arrive at the glinting
monument
to a westering migration.

There are untold
dark chapters
in the destiny

celebrated here,
the manifest one,
as we were taught.

Yet the form itself
I feel I need to meet
with my toddlers.

I work in a factory,
one that prints
news every day.

What's important
today is unimportant
tomorrow.

For now, I am
off the clock
and I hold

the children's
hands as
we approach.

A half-century on,
me and the arch,
I am back, pointing
my camera,
trying to capture
its whorl, its whispers.
I hear a faint summons.
I decide to look into
this with a different lens.

38.6251° N   90.1868° W

$$Y = A\left(\cosh\frac{X}{L}C - 1\right)$$

$$X = \frac{L}{C}\left[\cosh^{-1}\left(1+\frac{Y}{A}\right)\right]$$

Where, $A = \dfrac{f_c}{\dfrac{Q_b}{Q_t} - 1} = 68.7672$

$C = \cosh^{-1}\dfrac{Q_b}{Q_t} = 3.0022$

ξ = Max. Ht. of Centroid = 625.0925

Q_b = Max. X-Sec. @ Arch Base = 1262.6651

Q_t = Min. X-Sec. @ Arch Top = 125.1406

L = Half of Centroid @ Arch Base = 299.2239

866 tons of stainless steel
630 feet high, 630 feet wide

21

The arch men stacked triangular
wedges into a curled obelisk,
a clean line of chain bent
into lasting truth.

Sky writers, they hung
the essence upward
of people and planets,
our primal curves.

They wrote our name
across the sky,
distilled humanity
to its perfume.

I recognized
your voice, but not
your words.

Still you held on
to me, made me
feel belonging.

I left you,
but you stayed
with me.

Your foundation
and mine poured
the same summer.

I won't
let you go
again, brother.

Together, we
can sing a duet
to everyone.

Space in Man

Curled in his recliner,
the rocket scientist
fingered his slide rule,
calculating trajectories
for flying metal cans.

On his lap, charts, digits,
symbols, curves, arcs
he erased and redrew,
swiping eraser dust away,
ballistic sweeps rising.

As a boy, I could not
know the bearings
my father's pencil
would steer mine
eventually to.

Whispering Arch

There's craving in that curve still
at the old St. Louis train station.

The slightest whisper up one leg
of the big arch curls around clearly

to a listener far away at the other.
A vault to amplify tides of allure.

The secrets its eavesdropping
tiles must have tucked away,

a century of lovers, the fevers
of attraction, a crescent-full

of sweet nothings galloping within
a horseshoe big as a ballroom.

Priory Church

All that is light
all that is dark
all that is vault
all that is water

all that is origin
they all shape
the contours
of this stone realm.

A church on a hill.
Three tiers of arches,
concrete parabolas,
bent shadows of gravity.

Circular, its exterior
is black and white,
the shades of cosmos
older than color.

The walls wheel
with waves, as if
roused in a round
font for baptism.

Barely twelve,
I first steeped in
this shrine of
my boyhood school.

Fully immersed in one
another, this church
and I of the early '60s
shared our adolescence.

Decades on, I heard
the fluid form, the play
of dark and light here,
chanting . . . order

a harmony
of ripples echoing
into form all
over creation.

A trilogy
of arch tiers
schooled me
for a journey

Water Music

The clouds broke
for Luna today,
a year after her birth.

In a muddle-soup
of confusion, Luna
at last connected

that baritone,
that deep-voiced
other, with *dada*

and the taste of
teeth turned
to the taste of

her first word.
Before that, gurgles,
bubbles, dewdrops at play.

Like all infants,
Luna sprouted molars
just now, only after

her skull enlarged
enough for her jaw
to fully arch,

to house two ripe
parabolas, with molars
as the cornerstones.

Other primates race
molars in months earlier
as millstones for chewing.

Luna's molars needed
more time, to grind rice
and bread, and words.

Voice offers form
to the vapor of water,
the clouds we exhale.

Luna cut her teeth
on syllables stirring
in her little ears.

Through the arches
of her mouth, fog has
just begun to triumph

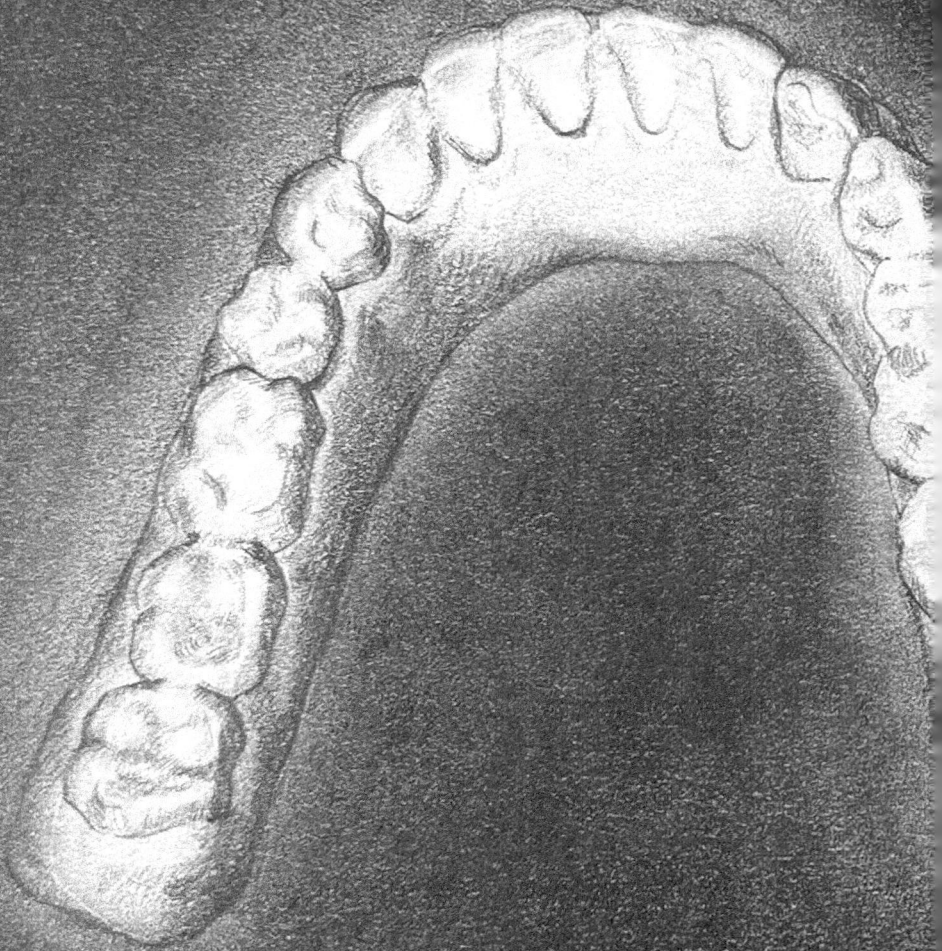

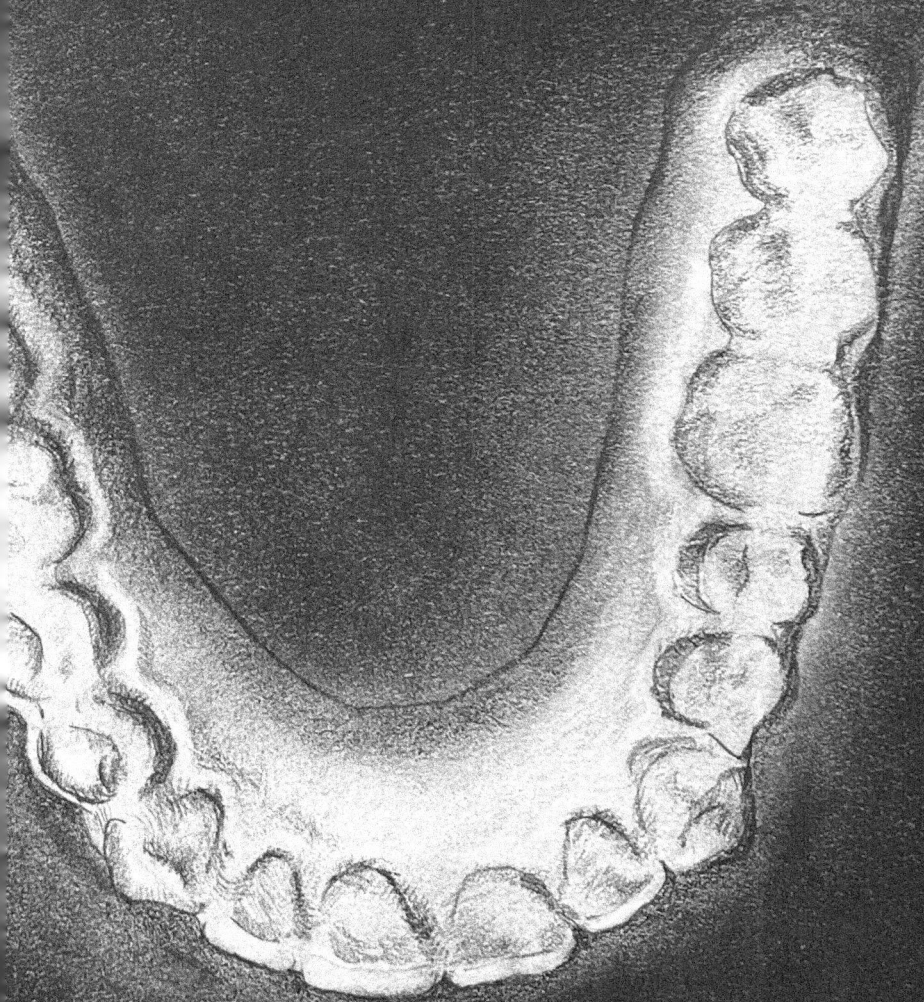

Brushstroke

Around two points
all parabolas
shape their lives.

Bent around
one focus
their arms

stretch to
the infinity
of the second.

Each focus
charms attracts
centers.

Focus comes
from Latin's *foci*
meaning hearth.

When the arches
behind lips
brush in a kiss

they stoke
fire,
and forever.

Hyperbola

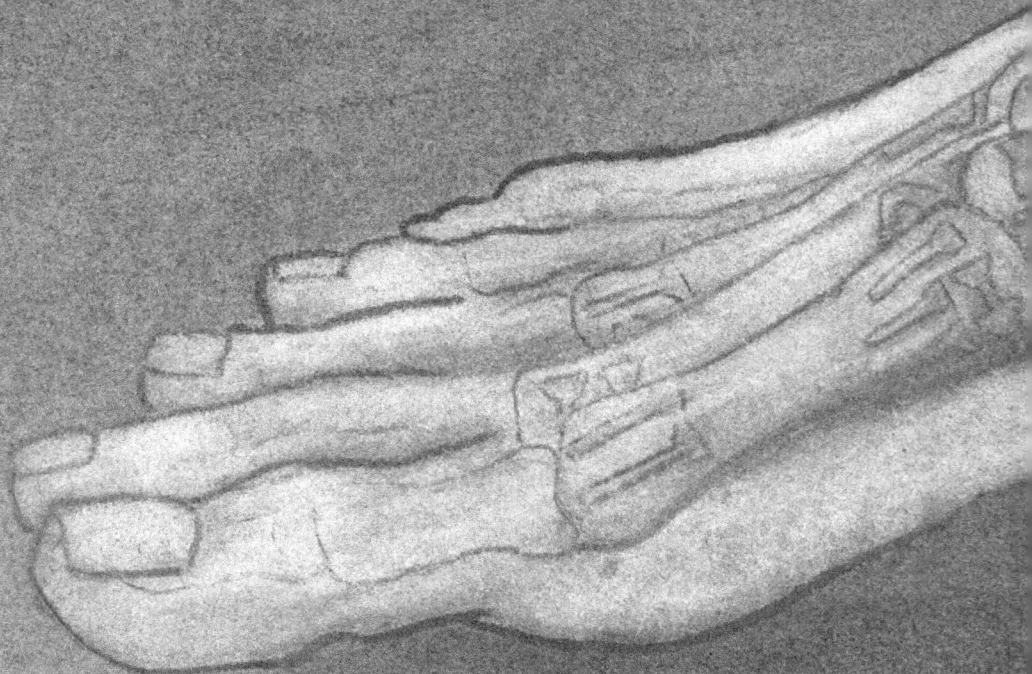

One Giant Leap

Feet write the epic
poem called humanity
marrow to marrow
over epochs
out of Africa
onto the moon

My Guitar

No one leads

in this dance.

We embrace

in a cloud

of chords.

Its sides are scooped

in hyperbolas,

like the arches

of my feet.

Who is

the instrument

in this soft promenade,

me or the guitar?

Gently, I step along

while my guitar,

my guitar gently walks.

Groundbreaking
moments,

how they
are sealed

in earth
rain and fire.

The oldest footprints
ever found.

Three early humans
out for a stroll.

Traipsing on
an unnamed

foot-shaped
continent.

Nearby a cone
of a volcano.

Three million years
ago, three humankinds

stepped along
a plain

in volcanic
tuff and ash

and rainfall,
feet pressing

a track of concrete
wells into fossil.

With finally upright
bodies, each being

an early tool
of penmanship,

a bone stylus
wedging into clay

the earliest script
the earliest cuneiform

as if to record
Here we are.

Finding the impressions
in Tanzania

in the 1970s
British archeologists

noted the toes
as close neighbors,

the human arches,
and they translated

what they read
into one word: *Us*

Lamplight

The living room lampshade casts
a perfect hyperbola
above and
below

below
and above
a perfect hyperbola
cast by the living room lampshade

Spiral Staircase

Built in a Santa Fe church
in the late 19th century

Wimpled, cloistral,
    the women prayed
        for these steps,

        steps that curl and spill
          in impossible geometry,
            chapel floor to choir

                loft, like some winding
                  flight through a lighthouse.
                  The stairs linger

                  in mystery after
                    an engineered century.
                      Their wood grain, still

                    unknown; their framework,
                    of a different architect.
                    In carved pirouettes,

                    the dervish whirls on
                    in the known, the unknown.
                    and the unknowing.

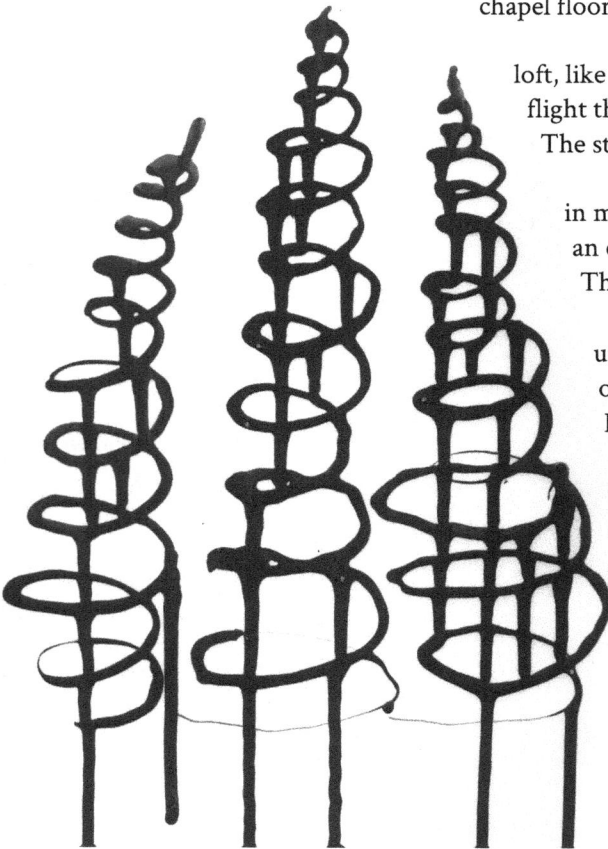

Beneath

Hours before he died, William Blake
called to his wife, anxious to draw
her portrait. It has since been lost.

How to describe the surface attacked
scraped and afflicted
the groove of your ashen
thumbnail forming her nape

your charcoal smudged in hatchings
swirls strokes blackening
your charcoal journeying
beneath likeness toward essence

Stay Kate
I will draw your portrait
keep just as you are
for you have ever been an angel to me

from your bedside you saw
her under her
woolen shawl rocking
with sore patient hands

and your practiced fingers
had traced the masters of old
had studied the underarchitecture
of muscle and bone

and you whose eyes saw holy
men shining through the ash-
caked coats of chimney sweeps
dug charcoal into that page

stirring embers
from dust and soot
a misty curvy gown
elbows bent blessedly

fingertips pressed in prayer
long liquid hair
wings between shoulders
a whole being floating

On My Birth Certificate

beneath name weight date,
blackened footprints.

When they lifted me from my cradle
to the form, they pressed left foot

where it said left, and right, right.
Ten dots for toes in two archipelagos,

and beneath, two continents,
a South America, an Africa.

Stretched across the dark lands
rivers branched, an Amazon, a Nile:

new clay imprinted with the mappings
of an earth those feet had yet to touch.

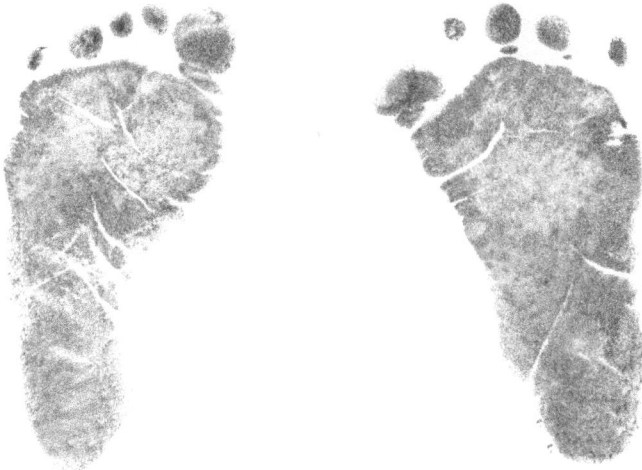

Spirit of St. Louis

Merry-go-round
of the Space Age
a groovy planetarium
tops a park hill

modern sculpture
aswirl as hyperbola
and parabola mounted
on forgotten stables

and all vantages
whisper *saddle*
inside this shrine
to the moon

we grade schoolers
skip around relics
Mercury and Gemini
space capsules

saddles made in our
own crossroads town
to carry men
pulses quickened

a hundred million
horses under them
nostrils fiery
hooves thundering

on a new ride
shrinking time, oceans
and space in a primal
reach for the sky

drawn to a light
that, as with us,
only reflects
a brighter source

On a vast figure eight
one Apollo rider
pointed a camera
over the moon

to find Earth, a blue
and white marble
in the black, coast
of Africa singing back

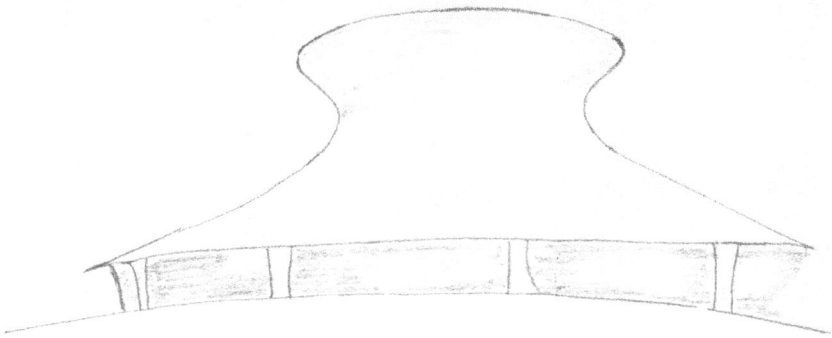

little redhead

flowers for eyes
my little brother
could not see

he could not
walk could
not speak

a dire virus
seized his
infant brain

wheeling
him around
my family

became his
feet his eyes
his voice

the shorelines within need
the rainfall within hands
the vineyards within smiles

not yet thirty
his life fading
his backbone

began bowing
shaping him into
a fetal crescent

a return
to everyone's
shared origin

a communion
with the curl
of new life

Ellipse

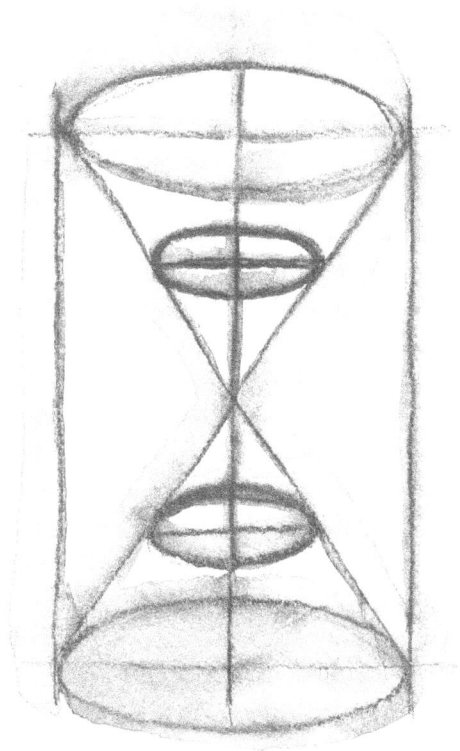

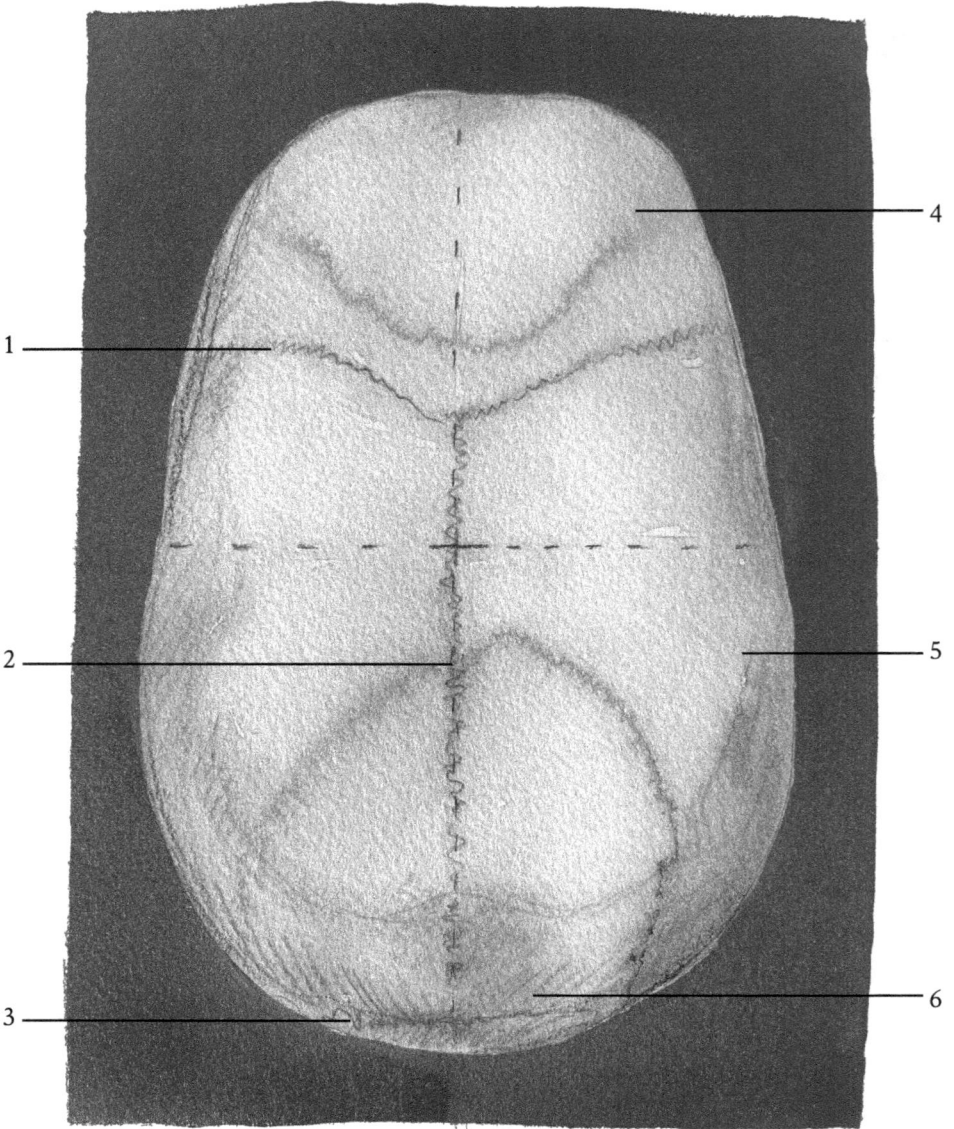

1. Coronal suture
2. Sagittal suture
3. Lambdoid suture
4. Frontal bone
5. Parietal bone
6. Occipital bone

Ode to Joy

Ring upon ring
the planets waltz
in a solstice festival,
worlds of presence
in absent space.

Trees radiate joy
in growth rings
presence absence
orbit on orbit
limb upon limb

early humans
nested in trees—
umbilical cords
sky to Earth—we
songs of the wood.

Joy circulates,
bend upon bend
into ova that amass,
swaddle new life,
shape belonging.

Kepler's Song

I tell you, we can measure
the weight of stars,
infinitesimal but surely
measurable, a dusting
of stellar heft on our flesh;
that we are stirred
and coaxed by thin light
piercing shadow.
I had searched, searched
    the far circles of the sky,
twisted concave mirrors until
night spilt into my bowls.
Then one night my fingers felt
a faint pressing—I turned
in the dark thinking
someone had breathed
on me. Then on my hand
I saw a spot of round light,
a drop of curd-pale moon.

Dust

The universe may be said
to be the original Adam,
a great body of dust,
organized into a system and
energized by the "breath" of God.
— Beatrice Bruteau

You can never
touch me twice;
in time, the whole
of me, outermost
is lost. As I walk,
old cells whirl
in a comet's tail.
Old me collects
in the corners.
Once me
in a dustpan.
Innermost,
new cells creep
from old depths
to the sheen,
to the sheen
of now me,
born inside out.

Mark Twain

Every star, unless it has a family of planets,
floats in an immeasurable solitude...

Handwritten note in
an astronomy book
the novelist owned

Born as Halley's Comet
crossed the night sky
you seemed so
homesick here

slinging stones
at a wandering river
called civilization
as if you were slung

in an orbit more
eccentric than
anyone on this world
more at home with rings

far larger than life
a misfit floating elliptically
on a raft called
lonely

schooling us in us
in black and white
until you passed away
at seventy-five just

as the comet returned
chalk dust in the night
leaving us yearning
for your glow to return

but faithful knowing
you would circle back
because as you told us
I been there before

Etch a Sketch

So many twisted blueprints:
skyscrapers, fences, chimneys.
You can lose yourself in a gray
maze that vanishes with a shake.

What a wonder in old times,
the red box with white knobs.
Twist one to scratch a line
horizontal; the other, vertical.

Curves are curious: the knobs
allow sideways or up and down,
but not around. So no room for
a moon, a breast, a smile.

The Discovery of Neptune

Too faint to see, but the law of loops
confirmed it's true, it must be there.

Newton and Kepler defined the ovals
of the geometric dance of the planets.

Then as the nineteenth century opened
explorers pointed their telescopes

to the far edge of the solar system,
a circling point of light called Uranus.

Tracking the planet, it seemed unruly,
riding a lopsided, not steady, oval track,

disturbed by something else, some neighbor,
a cousin tugging at it from the great beyond.

So a hunt began for an unidentified flying object,
one foretold by a constant called gravity.

With a quill pen, a Frenchman calculated
where the shadowy planet should be,

and sent his map to stargazers in Germany.
Within an hour, it lit up their telescope.

Your planet really exists, they wrote back.
Predicted by a pen, Neptune was found.

That telltale pen was a feather, as a bird
naturally knows the contour of an egg.

Heavengravel

Listen to this canyon,
the canyon where
it once rained bells.

Tongues of fire
split the sky, and
a boulder the size

of a blue whale
blazed down, a blast
furnace at landfall,

a thousand Hiroshimas
vaporizing vast forests,
mastodons, mammoths,

pulverizing stone, fusing
quartz into glass,
melting limestone, sandstone

into otherworldly taffy,
carving a mile-wide bowl,
a stadium of a crater.

The largest relic found:
a half-ton block of iron
long as your arm.

Dimples cover the silvery
fossil, and plum-size holes,
popped bubbles of inferno.

In now Arizona,
I am with this crater
and its meteorite.

Iron makes our blood
red, iron the mineral
of this meteorite.

I strike it with a marble
and the iron rings out,
a Buddhist temple bell.

The meteor is the message.
And I, I am struck
by this bell.

Wrinkled, with a pointy nose,
Ernst Chladni was a loner,
a little German physicist, he
arrived in the world with Mozart,
and departed with Beethoven.

With his violin bow,
the Father of acoustics
rendered sand paintings.
As he drew his horsehair rod
across a square brass plate,

vibrations from the bow
spread across the platter,
rattling grains of sand that
settled into intricate forms:
crosses, arabesques, ripples.

With his astounding musical act,
his name spread across
Europe, and Napoleon
invited him to perform
at the French palace.

His work made sound visible;
tempting nature, he said,
to expose itself. The first time
he tried, the grains orchestrated
into a star with ten rays.

Then Chladni moonlighted
on an entirely different mission:
to prove that streaks of light
in the night sky were actually
rocks falling from space.

The best minds in science then
thought the idea outlandish,
though the ancients used simple
eyesight to find stones, following
the flash paths to landfalls.

Inside pyramid walls,
hieroglyphics even revered
heavenly iron,
metal from meteorites
scavenged in Egypt.

Chladni eventually linked gravity,
planetary orbits, and meteors,
and gained another paternal title,
Father of shooting stars, making
meteors and sound siblings.

With his sand mandalas,
his sand madness, the violinist
sounded sand into ovals,
into spirals and arcs, struck upon
the structuring of the cosmos.

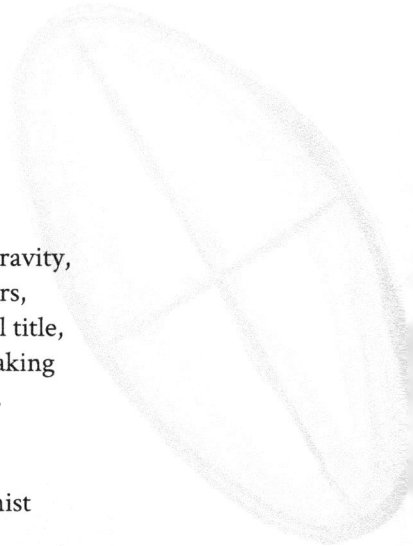

Cowboys, rock collectors,
and prospectors discovered
most of all the known
meteorites, whose elliptical
orbits collided with ours.

Crash-landing asteroids—
bigger meteorites—break
up, spewing remnants
into a large oval pattern,
an elliptical graveyard,

their beginning and end
formed in ellipses, these
immigrants of another world,
the old country they know
by heart.

near the beginning
when everything that is
was one vast dust cloud

waves of sound like notes
plucked from a harp
pulsed outward from

the original flaring forth
the birth of the universe
contractions that began

to coax the super cloud apart
waves the first form
rippling form through

the soup in a nocturne
a hymn a thousand
ages before any hymns

all of reality echoes
with the vibrato
of those early notes

plucks on a lyre
voicings of fire
sound before ears

that stirred
the fog of origin
fracturing

the colossal cloud
like Pangea
the supercontinent

into galaxies
whirlpools
twirling into someday

stars and planets
continents surrounded
by oceans of space

the shape of things to come
dust beckoning
twirling into someday

dust beckoning dust
all that is is vibrating
foremother notes linger

in spirals ovals
glorious arcs
prophecies

sent forth
going all along
song of songs

See his pointy harp
on the amphora,
the ochre man

in sunset tones
against the black
of the old Greek vase.

Orpheus the poet,
crowned with laurels,
plucking his lyre,

fingers spidery
across a web of strings,
serenading creation,

playing songs of such
light that trees and birds—
even stones danced.

He was known for
stirring the known world
to tremors with notes,

notes, form's first form,
like the cloud-splitting
vibes far ago in space.

Unheard trembling
reunited the cosmos,
saving it from chaos.

Things fall together,
it turns out,
the center can only hold.

And the myth
of Orpheus shows
the Greeks knew

in a way beyond
understanding that
all that is is vibrating,

that sound made order
of noise. That all that is
somehow rolls and swells.

All is waves, whether
light or heat or sound,
or billowing seas.

Orpheus sang and played
a parable of vibration,
of all the sounds we can

or cannot hear, or see,
the myth and voicings,
the oracle translated

now by scientists
into a dissonant vernacular
of sine waves and numbers.

Spirals

So exalting the glow
back then that anyone
could be enlightened by
the far circles of the sky.

Stone Age impressionists
left dreams in petroglyphs
spiral @ after spiral @
on every peopled continent

in someday Asia, Europe,
the Americas. So remote,
yet exhibiting one vision
abstract and otherworldly.

The people of a later
enlightenment
fogged in their burning
bulbs and chimneys

puzzled over the spirals on
megaliths and cave walls,
dismissing them as alien,
occult or rogue fantasy.

Now astronomers have found
our Milky Way galaxy is a spiral,
our sun one note among billions
on a curling musical score.

Our early ancestors carved
primal spirals knowing
beyond understanding
the composition of cosmos

spirals turning into ovals,
a new heavens, one starry
message after another echoing
one holy mantra. *Home.*

Seeds

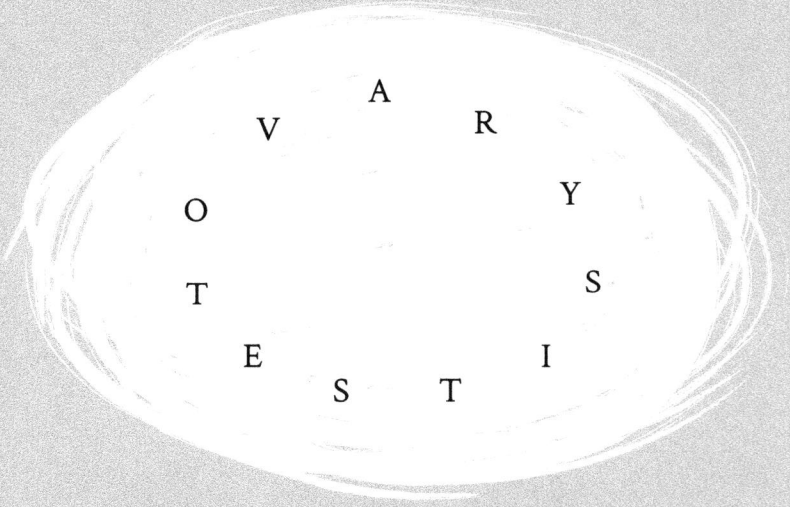

Cone

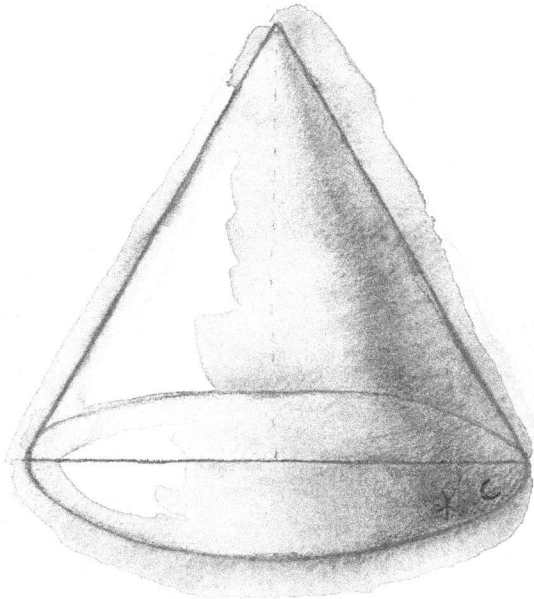

Teepee

Little mountain
in the wild

circle sloped
to a still point

hearth glows
within tent

pitched
against night

dwellers curled
under blankets

dreams, visions
and free

smoke
upward

churning
stars

chimney
downward

warm
this womb

this cone
of origin

of rhythm
and form

of union
and plan

Turning Triangle

From Euclid's Book 11

The cone
is a triangle
carried round
one fixed side and
restored again
to the same
position from
which it began
to be moved.

Findspot

A feast of threes
is served up on
this ceramic plate

handcrafted here
in Iznik, where it first
whispered to me.

Blue, white and red
fleurs-de-lis dance
with hearts and vines.

Land of antiquity,
land of threes, Iznik,
you bequeathed us:

Hipparchus the Greek
who held the sky
on his shoulders

and translated triangles
with an atlas now
called trigonometry.

Then, bishops who
met here when it
was called Nicaea,

forming a creed
around a mystery
called the trinity.

Over millennia,
over paths of art,
math, and faith

the vine of love
seems to beauty
forth in tercets.

Oracles

How their eyes could see deep
into tomorrows, into dawns,
these are the mysteries of Sámos.

So we are drawn to the emerald
Aegean, to this Greek isle, this
earth-shattering observatory.

Walk with me in the sandals
of Pythagoras, Aristarchus, and
an unsung muse we'll call Hera.

Pythagoras saw all of reality
as relation, a harmony voiced
in number, sung in triangle,

whether in music or planets, his
insights on connection founded
science, still unraveling all of this.

Aristarchus first cast the sun as
the center of all, not the earth,
correcting a grand illusion,

but when he moved humanity
off center stage, his play went
dark for over a thousand years.

Step now along the perfume
of oleander to those ruins,
the columned temple of Hera,

the goddess who once nursed
a deserted baby, milk spraying
out to form the Milky Way.

Losing my way, I see a fence.
A small schoolgirl, flowers for
eyes, greets me with *Yassou!*

Gathering her, I reply *Yassou!*
In her eyes fenceposts melt,
Hera in her temple.

Later that night above Sámos
I spot a bright speck roving
in the milk-speckled night,

the International Space Station,
a triumph of triangles, an isle
where lines dividing lands melt.

Let Us Make

Enter. Darkness. The horizon—see how it sharpens amid the afterglow.
Poets sometimes erase a few words from an existing poem to form
a new work from the remnants. Presence created by absence.
The center of gravity of every person funnels into an elegant
basin, the pelvis, the midpoint between head and foot.
As childhood fades, a shadow forms, a delta below
our hips, a remnant of fur unique among animals.
Presence created by absence. A pyramid
in sands of allure, a temple veil through
which we all pass, hip through hip,
a cloth of heaven perhaps,
or a tapestry of trinity.
Let us make
man in our
image
.

Sittings

How heavy the chin,
cornerstone of language.
Rodin's seated bronze

giant began as a tiny
door ornament.
His bearing grew into

The Thinker, buttressed
triangle upon triangle
—legs, arms, torso—

trussed to support
an arched megalith
called the jaw.

While sketching
The Last Supper,
Leonardo studied

Euclid's Elements
to illustrate a math book,
The Divine Proportion.

> *A triangular structure*
> *cannot change its shape*
> *under pressure or strain.*

In early Leonardo studies,
Jesus sat with his hands
upraised. Over time, he

became the centerpiece,
an equal-sided triangle,
one corner at his head,

the other two, his hands
resting on the table,
a calm base of stability.

With the triangle posing
as the artist's model,
anatomy melts

into now and any time,
beyond paint and ore,
into immortality

Over and Over

To be so at home
with the great
turning, the far
circles of the sky.
Along a great lake,
people gather nightly
in my town to look
west. Each sunset
a lullaby in oils.

Yesterday, I left home
for a different nocturne,
joining a great tide of
people, a tribe tugged
into a vision quest
into a larger path.
Distance offers abundant
shadows for searching
eyes to see new wholes.
We all knew just when
the eclipse would occur,
when our near star would
disappear in a cone of
night, and just where
the route would darken
along the turning globe.

Most comets arrive as
surprises, from a curl
thousands of years around,
but you can set clocks by
the spinning choreography
of the earth and the sun.
And the moon, we know,
from time to time cuts in.

My rendezvous with the great
shadow is on a playground.
Children twirl in place, dizzy
in laughter, spin on carousels.
A haze spreads. A summer
afternoon's heat wanes.
Not twilight now, not dusk,
not night. Some other side.
Birds stop chirping,
crickets start cricketing.
I keep watch through smoky
eclipse glasses. Bright truths
are the hardest to stare into.
Up above, all that is visible
now is a large pupil in a halo,
a ghostly eyeball. Absence
creating presence. Then
in a dazzling—flash—
night snaps back into
the day it just was.

I return home to sunsets
over the lake, the spinning
of children in a nearby park,
and crowds gathering nightly.
It's an endless bedtime story,
the seesawing of the sun
and the moon, and though
we know, we *know* how
the story goes
we want to hear it
over and over again

Grace and Gravity

Fall now with a fire not your own.
Sapling memories, veins draining,
wrinkled flesh, dew for breath,
a cloud with bones.

Nursed on light, you turned dawn
into life the color of pealing bells.
Cradled in skeletal boughs,
you unfolded. Stars swam

through lakes you held
in the sky. Let go now,
exhale in colors
the breath of sunset.

be

hold

Notes

5   Galileo Galilei and Stillman Drake, *Discoveries and Opinions of Galileo* (New York: Doubleday, 1957), 237-38.

53   Beatrice Bruteau, *God's Ecstasy: The Creation of a Self-Creating World* (New York: Crossroad, 1997), 15-16.

54   "Mark Twain Quotations," Mark Twain quotations, accessed September 28, 2024, http://www.twainquotes.com/. Credit to Twain scholar Barbara Schmidt.

Art by Kimberly Callas

Cover, *Behold,* India ink on paper, 9 x 12 in.

7   *Parabola,* water-soluble graphite on paper, 4 x 6 in.

15   *Arch,* Procreate digital drawing, 9 x 12 in.

30-31   *Sign Teeth,* graphite on paper, 12 x 16 in.

33   *Hyperbola,* water-soluble graphite on paper, 4 x 6 in.

34-35   *Cuneiform,* graphite on paper, 9 x 12 in.

40   *Watts,* India ink on Yupo paper, 9 x 12 in.

41   *Beneath,* water-soluble graphite and watercolor on paper, 9 x 12 in.

49   *Ellipse,* water-soluble graphite on paper, 4 x 6 in.

50   *Cranium,* graphite and charcoal on paper, 9 x 12 in.

52   *How the Stars Fell,* detail, powdered graphite and water-soluble graphite on Yupo paper, 9 x 12 in.

69   *Cone,* water-soluble graphite on paper, 6 x 6 in.

        Painted watermarks throughout the volume, water-soluble graphite on Yupo paper, 9 x 12 in.

Art by Michael McCarthy

26   *The Church,* graphite on paper, 8 1/2 x 11 in.

37   *Foot Notes,* cuneiform rendering of the poem title

43   *First Impression,* the author's newborn footprints, ink on Certificate of Birth, 9 x 6 in.

45   *Planetarium,* graphite on paper, 8 1/2 x 11 in.

70   *Conic Sections,* laser-cut pressboard sculpture, with templates by mathhappens.org, 6 x 6 in.

        All photographs in this volume, except the St. Louis Arch photo with the author as a boy and his sisters on page 20, by Carlisle McCarthy, Michael's father

Interior Design by Jody Langley

www.ingramcontent.com/pod-product-compliance
Lightning Source LLC
Chambersburg PA
CBHW060323070426
42446CB00049B/2302